Love For The Chubby Women.

Get to know chubby women like never before.

Jane Logan

Table of contents

Introduction.

All is fair in love and war, they say.

It doesn't make any difference in the event that you're fat or slim when you love. Since affection doesn't zero in on the presentation but on the magnificence of your spirit inside.

For the people who disdain tubby young ladies, it could be an unexpected treat for them that somebody can entirely be blissful and chubby.

Chubby ladies aren't really hung up on looks and are bound to give up and live it up with you once they figure out that you're cheerful being with them.

Truth be told, nothing about a tubby young lady's appearance make them dishonorable of extraordinary love, great sex, and regard.

Chapter 1

Things you probably didn't know about chubby women.

If you are a chubby individual in the world today, you understand what segregation feels like. This segregation isn't generally self-evident assuming you don't have the foggiest idea of what to search for. It is the looks you get as a chunky individual eating anything that isn't healthy. It's the trouble you face finding sexy outfits, the remarks from companions who are consuming fewer calories while complaining that they are "so fat" when they are skinnier than you, the worry from the family that you would look "so much more pleasant" if you were to shed a couple of pounds. This is fatphobia, characterized as the trepidation and scorn of fat bodies.

Bringing issues to light.

At the point when chubby individuals examine fatphobia, they are frequently met with the abnormal quiet of doubt or dissent from the individual you're testing; they don't detest hefty individuals; they're only "worried about your wellbeing." Be that as it may, there is a rising spotlight on fatphobia on stages like Instagram, Tik-Tok, and even Twitter, as individuals share their encounters and show how fatphobia appears in ways that are frequently ignored, from abuse over physical qualities to uncontrolled eating regimen culture.

There is extremely restricted research on fatphobia and its impact on youngsters. This might be, to some extent, due to the fact that research on this topic seldom sees explicit encounters, and because youngsters rarely talk about it. However, youngsters are normally more helpless against separation, for example, fatphobia, and this is the sort of thing that we as an exploration bunch knew well.

Long-lasting effect.
Having seen and experienced fatphobia, we needed to utilize our foundation to show that the issues chubby individuals face in the public eye today are genuine and influence them until the end of their lives.

Through our examination and encounters, we fostered a study that addressed a couple of areas of society in which fatphobia can show. We accumulated 36 respondents who matured somewhere in the range of 16 and 25. Most members are recognized as female, with non-double individuals making up the second-biggest orientation character in our information. Male came third, and genderqueer made up our most unaddressed orientation character.

Key Findings.

Members featured that fatphobia starts to show right off the bat throughout everyday life. Remarks from relatives about weight brought about members seeing themselves adversely. One respondent said:

"My family remarked on my weight before I was even fat. They gave me a complex about my weight [...] and it gave me an undesirable relationship with food and with my body."

Respondents likewise shared their negative encounters with medical services, with 69% of members saying they had experienced clinical fatphobia, and many saying they were denied further examinations because of their size.

The profoundly imbued nature of fatphobia inside society has brought about numerous people seeing their bodies adversely because of their weight. That's what one respondent announced:

"I've been caused to feel like I am not a decent individual and not deserving of adoration, consideration, or understanding due to my weight."

Handling segregation.

The discoveries give an understanding of youngsters' encounters with fatphobia. What's more, as youngsters ourselves, we had the option to embrace a significant exploration project, regardless of whether it isn't the most famous or handily comprehended. We have had the option to focus light on segregation and give youngsters a stage to share their encounters - as well as give a valuable chance to contemplate how fatphobia shows and how it can be handled.

A thick and chubby individual has had to deal with a ton currently, particularly in the present culture. We live in a culture that characterizes them as unfortunate, an issue, revolting, and unclean.

Thus, if you like a thick lady at any moment, ensure you are not kidding about getting to know her. The B.S., furthermore, the disillusionments she has looked at in the past are sufficient. There are a lot of things you should realize that ought to urge you to cherish them.

1. *They are enchanting.*

The greater part of the rotund young ladies wears a grin all over all the time without fail. You'll get an inspirational tone with them which is astonishing. They will facilitate your weight and you'll feel lighter with them around. They'll capture your consideration after the main gathering itself.

2. *They are nice.*

Fatigue will evaporate from your word reference on the off chance that you date a sound lady. You can converse with them about anything as their relational abilities are perfect. Since they scarcely care about external looks, they have a sharp and visionary brain.

3. *Warmth.*

Thin young ladies couldn't draw near to the glow and simple inclination that a plump young lady gives. While you may not think that she is sufficiently alluring, you won't find the adoration and warmth like her with any other individual. Their glow can in a split second illuminate your temperament.

4. *Love for food.*

Indeed, food is bae and if you love food, investigating new food joints, and attempting new things, a rotund young lady is the best partner. They are generally up to trying new things which you'll understand when you begin to spend time with them. She is distraught, daring, and energetic.

5. *They are easy to read.*

Husky young ladies could do without insider facts. Assuming she bonds with you, she'll open up with you sharing all that is in her heart. They snicker at the issues as opposed to getting miserable. Their uplifting outlook will make you hopelessly enamored with her considerably more. They are diverting and know how to manage your temperament changes. Young men are expected to spoil their women yet for this situation, it will be the alternate way round!

6. *Continuously dynamic and lively.*
Whether you need to go on an excursion or climbing or water sports, she would constantly be prepared to go with you. Try not to go by their well-being and physical make-up, they are more dynamic and enthusiastic than different young ladies.

7. *Tender.*
A hefty young lady cherishes long embraces, steady nestles, and a wide range of heartfelt emotions. Give her adoration and she'll respond with endless warmth. If you are somebody who loves her young lady to be friendly, date a

tubby young lady. She'll bring heaps of tomfoolery, experience, love, and energy into your life.

When you approach them completely furnished with this information, you'll urge them to act naturally around you. The following are four things that are similarly significant for you to be familiar with dating a thick lady:

1. *Try not to make them the aim of a joke.*

At the point when you date a thick lady, ensure you are not kidding.

Try not to date her if you simply have any desire to embarrass her. Try not to engage with her if you only want to give her a shot since she's "huge in the appropriate spots".

These reasons are very dehumanizing and destructive for them. Most thick ladies foster trust issues concerning anybody's capacity to adore them.

2. *Be ready to get undesirable thoughts.* Rotund young ladies explore in a work that continually tells them of their disgracefulness. It implies that regardless of how sure they will be, they are as yet exposed to demonstrating their value. You might meet the surest rotund young lady on the planet however it wouldn't change the way that the general public will attempt to persuade them that they ought to can't stand themselves.

Rotund young ladies need backing to flourish. If you like a plump young lady, give her security and care. Try not to cause her to feel remorseful for abusive excellence principles that you have zero power over.

3. *Be cautious with underhanded commendations.*
An underhanded commendation is a comment which is by all accounts a commendation but is intended to be an affront.

The best illustration of this is the point at which a man says: "I love a lady with meat on her bones." it might sound empowering but when you consider it, it is stripping you down to carnal substantiality.

Sadly, this is the most widely recognized conversation starter for individuals who need to play with a rotund young lady. It harms because nobody needs to hear that your reason for needing them is because you're not interested in another person.
Sexualizing, fetishizing, and racializing chubby ladies convey dehumanization and viciousness behind it.

If you value her, simply tell her straight.

"You're alluring to me."

"You're commendable."

"You are more than your body, however, I love valuing your excellence."

4. *Be ready to challenge fatphobic assumptions for your relationship.*
When in a relationship with a rotund young lady, there are a few things you can't do if you weigh not as much as her. You're most likely not going to do that charming piggyback thing couples do in motion pictures.

Likewise, the principles of physical science express that you can't get her and convey her in your arms assuming she falls and damages her lower leg during a zombie end of the world.

So before you get into a relationship with a tubby young lady, be ready to contemplate them. Contemplate the estimating of seats in cafés or arenas, how she can't wear your garments, how you travel (transport, train, or plane, what sort of bed we get, and so on.).

It makes a difference since it implies you are contemplating the way that you can be a decent sweetheart to her.

Chapter 2

Loving yourself as a thick woman.

Dearly adored peruser, I will be genuine with you as I share with you a couple of privileged insights of "Curvy Women Who Love Their Bodies."

The main inquiry that I get posed as a self-perception master and chubby lady who cherishes her body is: How did you make it happen?

Frequently there's some assumption that an enchanted mixture or being brought into the world on a mysterious unicorn-pervaded (swarmed?) the island is essential for the story. However, my mystery in adoring my body is simply how it is. All things considered, I'll give it to you in a moment. Guarantee!

When I first met a breathtaking lady who cherished her body I was presumably in 6th grade.

Mrs. Carlyle wore business skirts and silk pullovers, and the trim of her slip was scarcely noticeable through the little cut at the back. She amended youngsters' spelling with this sort of cruel enjoyment. She didn't walk. Sweetheart sauntered.

What's more, at age eleven, she altered how I saw my future unfurling.

Very nearly twenty years after the fact, Mrs. Carlyle's walk examples long neglected, I was welcome to go to a fat gathering in Berkeley, San Francisco.

I strolled in and saw a curvaceous lady in a spotted one-of-a-kind one-piece swimming outfit. She had huge shades on, and a charming kid was holding a parasol for her so she wouldn't get burned by the sun.

Astounding style (and parasol pool kid) aside, it was her finished absence of reluctance - her easily nonchalant, yes-I'm-the-most smoking thing-since-cinnamon-toast demeanor - that truly struck me.

She had knocked my socks off by simply doing her thing: it was delightful to lounge around knowing her. She turned into the permanent picture of what body love resembled me. I needed to know her mystery.

Why Body Love Is the Most Important Part of a Balanced Existence.

Consistently, ladies (perhaps you?) awaken, and the primary thing that they consider is the way that their bodies don't compare to a generally media-produced picture of ladylike excellence.

We are educated to think with regards to a future self: "Twenty pounds from now, I will wear that short skirt. Thirty pounds from now, I will want to appreciate checking myself out in the mirror. Forty pounds from now, I will adore this body."

We lose valuable minutes and stretches of life to these untruths.

(Indeed, I said it: lies.)

At the point when we live from now on, we lose this point.

Three of my most profoundly held convictions are:

- Each body is a decent body.

- Wellbeing is comprehensive, and psychological well-being is a gigantic piece of all-encompassing wellbeing.

- Self-loathing is a philosophy that can be destroyed through an act of confidence.

Everybody is qualified for a relationship with their body that is situated in care and regard. In this way, now is the right time to quit considering your body is a threatening encasing in which you are detained. You're not a detainee. You're a visitor at a 5-star inn, young lady!

Absorb the wisdom from 8 women who talk about the keys to their body love.
I requested answers from the most marvelous stunning ladies that I know.

First inquiry: What is the large confidentiality of your relationship to your body?

Their responses are as follows:

1. Tanya, The Body Is Not An Apology.
"My large confidence in my relationship with my body is advising myself that my body isn't the adversary.
"In any event, when I'm debilitated, feeling yucky is a sign of my body striving to return to wellbeing. That fever? Correct, only my body forcing sickness to leave!

"My body is my ally! It believes that I should have areas of strength for feeling, and be cheerful.

At the point when I permit myself to register with this reality, it makes space for me to have genuine sympathy for my body.

"In any event, when I'm not feeling fabulous, I can return to realizing that my body is working with me, not against me. It's my best partner in living my fullest in a festival of extremist confidence!"

2. Martha, Riots Not Diets.
"I wear garments that fit well, no matter what the size recorded on the tag, in styles and varieties that encourage me.

"I toss out every one of the principles about what I 'should' wear, and style my body in a dress that appeals to me. It's most certainly extreme to find hefty size garments that work, yet it's certainly feasible - and I never love my body more than while I'm shaking my #1 outfit.

"(Or on the other hand when I'm absolutely stripped - that is amazing, as well!)"

3. Tina, Fat, Smart, and Pretty.
"There is no such thing as my largeness in a vacuum. Individuals care about my chubby body since we have made these imperceptible designs like free enterprise, sexism, and imperialism that show us what bodies are great and what bodies are terrible. The issue is, they're off-base.

"Many long stretches of mankind's set of experiences misunderstand the chubby woman. The justification for why individuals generally dislike my body isn't on the grounds that my body is awful. It is important to know there is no incorrect method for having a body.
"So rather than lashing out at my body for not squeezing into the slender ideal, I

let myself fly off the handle at omnipresent but anonymous rich, white men who have made these social designs.

"That outrage frequently lights my assurance to wear a tank top and gladly show my fat arms and furry armpits. Truth be told, rich, white men: take a gander at my body and be apprehensive."

4. Gina, Gina the Great.
"Get exposed to yourself. Begin at the top and work your direction down, feeling your whole body as you go. Set aside some margin to pause and inspect parts you feel new to.

"Become familiar with your body. Stretch imprints, knicks, hair, lopsided shading, wrinkles. Spread your butt in the mirror. Sniff your own armpits. Snatch your stomach. Taste yourself.

Second inquiry.

"You don't become companions with somebody by simply checking them out. You really try to get to know them, and over the long run, they become a wellspring of commonality and solace. Your body can possibly be your BFF."

5. Cara, Curvy Girl Inc.

"One day when I was around 22, I concluded life is excessively short to require all that to be postponed until I am the media's meaning of the ideal weight. (I had lost my closest companion since the 3rd grade. That awakened me.)

"Our bodies, even our fat bodies, are prepared to do lots of delightful things. Your lover is there and exposed with you at this moment. Not fifteen pounds from now.

"My speculation is there's nothing that can be done about it. If not, how could they be there bare with you?

"Have a go at moving around in a yummy bed or take a decent warm, foamy shower with another breathtaking lady (or man) and shut your eyes and just let your hands feel their delicate skin, rolls, and heavy aspects and perceive how extraordinary their body feels to the touch.

"You will have another appreciation for how wonderful your body is."

6. Linda, Linda Adams.

"I love ceremonies, and one of the main customs of my life is to saturate in the first part of the day.

"Not just because my wonderful earthy-colored skin is more appealing with cream, but since I get to feel every last bit of my body. Gradually. Pleasantly. Delicately. Affectionately.

"It's a course of valuing each inch, each cell, each blemish, and every last trace of flawlessness.

"This cycle likewise advises me that I am violating such a huge amount in orientation, sexuality, and recovering femme for myself as a brown trans lady."

7. Anna, The Sex Positive Parent.
"My biggest mystery is that I love having a major body. I realize we should stand it. Each lady should wish she was more modest and humble and to take up the minimal measure of room conceivable, however, I don't.

"I love that I'm bigger than my sweethearts. I love realizing that my thighs are thicker than theirs. It's a mystery since it makes me sound cutthroat or bossy. In any case, my thighs are bossy - they tell you precisely what they believe that you should improve, not sass them.

"My shoulders are bossy, as well. I can get what I need when I need it. I can disregard you or embrace you with these large-ass shoulders.

"It's something beyond not being embarrassed about being huge. I love it."

8. Kate, Purr Versatility.
"The greatest mystery to my relationship with my body came when I fostered my very own wild feeling style.

"It was generally difficult to dress marvelously for my shape. I had almost no direction, scarcely any style symbols, and close to zero shops to peruse in or explore different avenues regarding. I needed to foster an extremely toughness as 'husky young lady' clothing stores let me down with their restricted determination.

"At last, I sorted out a method for breaking out of the shape, wearing garments that express my character well and look complimenting on my figure.

"What's more, it's positively repetitive: When I feel like I've arranged an astounding look, I feel astonishing in my body, which makes it simpler to pull off more out-of-control styles!"

Your Body Love Homework.

Before I give you your schoolwork, I guaranteed you I'd give you my mystery. It's straightforward.

Yes!

The key to my relationship with my body is that I get up each day and say OK.

Indeed to this stomach, yes to these boobs, yes to these chubby cheeks and this tubby life.

Indeed to cupcakes, to short dresses that let me feel the breeze against my thighs, to this twofold jaw that shakes when I chuckle.

Indeed to dates with cuties who realize this body is awesome, yes to husky young lady photograph shoots, yes to cleavage and pencil skirts, and yes to the mysterious radicalism of my reality.

Indeed, body, I will cherish you since that is precisely the exact thing you merit and in light of the fact that it's so extraordinarily fun.

Alright, would you say you are prepared for that schoolwork?
Record five things your body has accomplished for you recently. At the present time. It very well may be anything from "looked charming in that sweater" to "processed toward the beginning of today's oat without a blip."

Then, at that point, see that rundown and understand that it very well may be quite a bit longer.

That rundown can be the most important phase in the extreme re-imagining of your relationship to your body.

Body love is the best gift you can give yourself. In this way, young lady, get to wrapping.

Chapter 3

Why being with a thick woman is better.

A ton of men don't consider chubby young ladies to be their partners due to a few reasons. They are not viewed as ideal dating material on account of their body estimations. In any case, you would be shocked to realize that plump, solid, or larger estimated ladies have preferred partners over the rest! Having a chubby young lady close by has various advantages which you'll come to be aware of.

1. Science Says So!

After so many experiments have been carried out by experts, it was figured out that thick young ladies ordinarily have more endorphins created in their cerebrum, because of that fine layer of fat under their skin. Endorphins, otherwise called feel-great synthetic compounds, are straightforwardly connected to satisfaction, solace, unwinding, and even happiness. This multitude of mental qualities permits chubby young ladies to appreciate better sex. As you most likely are aware, a peaceful psyche is crucial to living it up in bed.

2. More Scientific Evidence.

Some time back, scientists at a certain university in the UK led an assessment review and sorted out that most members (guys) needed to have a thick lady in their bed over more slender ones. The explanation is self-evident, and we as a whole know it! It isn't only consistently about sex; chubby ladies draw in men quickly with their enormous resources concealed under close outfits! Disregard those logical examinations; most folks on famous web-based networks like Reddit say they find sex with a chubby young lady more pleasurable than a skinnier one.

3. Thick Girls Have Got More Cushion Down There!

If you are a thin fellow and banged a dainty young lady previously, you probably know how difficult the extraordinary stroking meeting is. It doesn't feel extraordinary when two hard pelvic areas slap hard against one another. Young ladies with bends have a little tissue of fat simply over their "woman fix" that goes about as a pad, permitting men to stroke all the more with great intensity. Their large goods give the perfect sort of cushioning folks need during positions like doggie to make things simple and pleasurable. This large number allowed men to stroke harder and more profoundly, assisting ladies with accomplishing serious climaxes.

4. There Is More To Explore!

The body of a chubby lady is exceptionally entrancing. It has more surface region, and that implies, there are a lot of secret fortunes to investigate! Their bigger bosoms, greater goods, substantial thighs, soft paunch, and so forth are an outright treat to watch, contact, and stroke. Having intercourse with a chubby lady allows a man's body to come into complete contact with hers. Individuals think that it is alleviating and truly agreeable. There are administrations offered where thick young ladies give full body-to-body messages. As you probably are aware, most folks have a serious fixation for enormous booties, and obviously, just thick young ladies have them!

5. Butt And Boob Jiggles Make Men Go Mad.

A thick young lady's body is fluidic. The pieces of hers move alongside each stroke or push. Be it the preacher position, the young lady on top, or the doggie, each attractive move sends swells across her body. Presently, this is a profoundly sensual sight, and it makes most men go distraught. Having an insane person in bed consequently guarantees unusual things to occur, which further prompts an exceptionally remunerating hot time. The sound a major run makes when slapped into a man's pelvis drives a man as well as his partner insane.

6. Thick Girls Are Confident.

Chubby young ladies are generally body positive, and they are never irritated by their enormous size. They eat what they need, and don't starve themselves. Thick young ladies scarcely care about individuals' thought processes of them, and they generally convey a healthy identity confirmation. Try to recollect a chubby young lady you know, and we bet she is quite possibly the most confident young lady you at any point met! They show their certainty even in bed and won't hesitate to flaunt what they have. Chubby young ladies understand what their assets are, and they set out to utilize every one of them to satisfy their men!

7. Big Boobs.

We should discuss significant things now! Except for a couple of sad ones, most chubby young ladies have enormous boobs. As you probably are aware, boobs are a rare example of erogenous female body parts. Most young ladies love it when their partners stroke or suck them for a more extended period. Men, then again, love large boobs. It's anything but confidential, and everybody knows their fixation on bigger bosoms. Huge bosoms permit folks to invest more energy in foreplay, consequently permitting the sexual experience to remain longer. As you probably are aware, a dependable and extreme sex meeting is more compensating to ladies than men.

8. Booty.

Boobs or goods? Numerous men find this question challenging to respond to except if they question back by saying, "why not both?!" A major and alluring butt is something each lady wants to have. It is an exemplary component of a chubby young lady. Any man who loves to play with a full and round derriere simply has to date a chubby young lady! Comparatively like enormous boobs, major goods increments sex time. Men like to invest energy "adoring" the intriguing ladylike region. Ladies love anything men do to their backs, as the butt is likewise one of the erogenous pieces of a female body.

9. They Endure Long And Intense Sexual Encounters.

Chubby ladies are very much assembled and have sound bones and muscles. They have significantly more endurance than dainty young ladies. This permits chubby young ladies to take part in extreme focus and energy-depleting sexual experiences. They don't feel tired or lose interest rapidly, and this is the kind of thing most men love to find in a lady. These ladies needn't bother with a lengthy recuperation period after sex. Folks fixated on sex frequently find their typical constructed sweethearts cry in torment or weak during the demonstration. On the off chance that you assume you are a superman of sex, look no further and invite a breathtaking chubby lady home!

10. Thick Girls Are Less Judgmental.

Most thick young ladies are not critical because they could do without living fair and square. They couldn't care less about body norms. A hot and zero-size chick might dismiss your adoration referring to your wellness levels as an explanation, yet a thick young lady is less inclined. Surprisingly, chubby ladies are generally undemanding, and they are probably the most amicable individuals you can at any point meet. You may need to date a plump young lady to know how extraordinary they are sleeping and how pleasant they are personally.

11.They Are Great Cuddlers.

Snuggling is something all ladies love to do. However men don't straightforwardly discuss it, they love to get in the bed and cuddle with the other gender too. Chubby ladies are extraordinary cuddlers, and laying down with them causes one to feel extremely loose. By the way, there are administrations where men get to cuddle and lay down with a cuddly lady. Having a thick young lady return home for a sleepover can be an extremely fulfilling experience. Do you need a decent night's rest? Date a plump young lady, then!

12. Men Find Sex With Curvy Girls Addictive.

Haven previously educated you on why thick young ladies are perfect in bed, this comes as no surprise. I have explained their body, their demeanor, and numerous different things. On account of those, men as a rule find rotund young ladies habit-forming, particularly sex with them. Presently this implies that chubby ladies get sex more habitually than a typical young lady!

* * * * * *

More often than not, chunky ladies experience both the shame of ugliness and the disgrace they need control. They are unfairly judged in light of their looks and sizes as opposed to their keenness. They are seen as feeble and lethargic.

They get prodded even by outsiders because of their well-being, which is more terrible than prodding. 'Who will wed you' is a typical insult flung at them.

Though wedding a chubby young lady is a personal decision for some reasons. Yet, another review proposes that men who wed chubby ladies will quite often have a peaceful life.

Men who wedded a hefty young lady will quite often grin more and be greater at managing issues than men in associations with flimsy ladies.

People with Responsive Partners Experience Lower Uneasiness, Better Rest Quality.

Chubby ladies are bound to expect their partner's necessities. They make their men multiple times as blissful as slim ladies which make them (men) have a more extended life.

www.ingramcontent.com/pod-product-compliance
Lightning Source LLC
LaVergne TN
LVHW020526160826
845677LV00015B/3934

* 9 7 9 8 3 5 1 7 1 7 9 8 2 *